E - ENJOY HIS PRESENCE

BOOK 2 IN THE "REMAIN" SERIES

DART EASTWOOD

INTRODUCTION

In John 15:4-5 Jesus tells us, "Remain in Me, and I in you. Just as the branch cannot bear fruit of itself but must remain in the vine, so neither can you unless you remain in Me. I am the vine, you are the branches; the one who remains in Me, and I in him bears much fruit, for apart from Me you can do nothing."

This REMAIN series seeks to help us to deepen our relationship and walk with Jesus. Dart's transparency in these books helps guide and encourage us to focus on following God, seeking His will, and trusting His love for us so we can in turn love ourselves and love others. Each book has its own focus...

E - Enjoy His presence daily... the sky, mountains, flowers, birds, children. (Psalm 8) This 2nd collection in the REMAIN series invites you into the joy of receiving the blessings of His love every day, in all the small, beautiful gifts He uniquely showers on each of us.

FINDING FAITH IN THE FERTILIZER

SOMETIMES BEING BURIED IN "CRAP" IS A GOOD THING!

"The grass is always greener on the other side of the fence."

I know we've all heard this a million times...

Our husband (or kids or friends or family or boss or - fill in the blank!) doesn't appreciate us the way we think they should. Especially not the way THAT woman's husband (or kids or friends or family or boss or ...) does.

Our home is too small, or too far from town, or too close to the street, or doesn't have enough bathrooms, or a big enough yard. THAT house over THERE would be PERFECT!

We're unhappy in our job and we think it would be better if we quit and went to work for another company. In another industry. In another town. In another state. In another country. Anywhere but HERE.

We're miserable HERE, and it MUST be better THERE.

I once had a neighbor, Sandy, who had THE most amazing yard E-VER. Seriously. I'd look at the withered, brown, crunchy grass on my side of the fence and I'd long for my lawn to be lush and green and soft and inviting. Like the lawn over THERE. In Sandy's yard. If I could just get to over THERE, I would be happy. I could lie in the sweet tender grass and relax in the warmth of the golden sunshine that seemed to only shine in Sandy's yard.

Over THERE.

Clearly, I was missing something.

Finally, I humbled myself and asked Sandy how she got her yard to be so beautiful. She listed all the same things I was doing in my yard... the watering, the weeding, the aerating... and then she said something I hadn't thought of before. She used fertilizer. Fertilizer??!! DUH!!! I felt so stupid! *sigh*

She gave me the name of a brand and I immediately picked some up and sprinkled it all over my lawn just the way she instructed. Within a couple months my lawn was green and lush and gloriously magnificent!! All because of fertilizer!! WhoooHooooo!!!! It was awesome!!

One day, several years later, I was grumbling to God (again!) about something in my life and how "it would be SOOOO much better if..." The Lord gently said to me, "Find faith in the fertilizer."

Uuuuuhhhhhhmmmm....

What??

I had absolutely NO idea what He was talking about, so I forced myself to sit down and be quiet for a little while so I could hear Him speak more clearly on this subject. Suddenly a memory of my beautiful lawn of long ago drifted through my thoughts. I remembered how lush and green it was after I'd started using the fertilizer... but I was still confused by what exactly the Lord was trying to get me to understand. How do you have faith in fertilizer??

"What is fertilizer?" He asked me.

My first thought was the "scientific" blend of teeny-white-popcorn-ball lawn fertilizer I'd used per Sandy's instructions, but He said, "No, no... more basic than that." Well... the most "basic" fertilizer I can think of is manure. Horse manure. Cow manure. Bunny poop. Chicken poop. Goat poop. Composty poop. That's right. A bunch of crap...

It's completely natural but... it's stinky... and unpleasant... and, it's no fun to STEP in, let alone be buried in! But, it's great for the soil! It actually changes the chemical makeup of the earth and brings it into balance. It makes it healthy. Where things can grow.

I felt Him smile as His message began to take root in my heart.

We all have "crap" in our life that we don't like to deal with... all the stuff we think of as "waste." We think we're in the wrong job or the wrong marriage or car or house or city or discussion or YEAR! We think if we just got out of these stinky, unpleasant situations our life would be sooo much better.

Even when we feel completely buried by it all, God told us He will never give us more than we can bear, (1 Corinthians 10:13) but only because He doesn't expect us to bear it alone! It IS too much for us to bear if we try to do it WITHOUT Him. 2 Corinthians speaks of the incredible trials that Paul endured, but he said it was in order "that we might not rely on ourselves but on God." (2 Corinthians 1:8-9)

Some situations ARE toxic and dangerous and you DO need to get out of them, but those are pretty rare. Instead of escaping the "fertilizer" in our life, what if we allowed it to change us? What if we worked through the yuck - with God! - and allowed the crap to actually change OUR makeup and bring US into balance, just like the manure does for the earth? What if that's why God allows these things to happen? What if we trusted Him in it? What if the "fertilizer" actually helps drive us into His arms and increases our reliance on Him instead of ourselves?

It still feels like crap and it still stinks, but, I'm starting to understand what He meant when He said to find faith in the fertilizer. It's not the fertilizer I find faith in… it's finding my faith in God while I'm IN the fertilizer of my life. The grass is greener where there's plenty of water, sunshine, AND fertilizer.

In Jesus' name.

Amen.

SCRIPTURES

1 Corinthians 10:13 - No temptation has overtaken you that is not common to man. God is faithful, and he will not let you be tempted beyond your ability, but with the temptation he will also provide the way of escape, that you may be able to endure it. (ESV)

2 Corinthians 1:8-9 - For we do not want you to be uninformed, brethren, about the affliction and oppressing distress which befell us in the province of Asia, how we were

so utterly and unbearably weighed down and crushed that we despaired even of life itself. Indeed, we felt within ourselves that we had received the very sentence of death, but that was to keep us from trusting in and depending on ourselves instead of on God Who raises the dead. (AMPC)

FIX YOUR FOCUS

WHATEVER WE FOCUS ON BECOMES STRONGER... SO FIX YOUR FOCUS ON THE RIGHT THINGS!

Key Scripture ~ Matthew 14:29-32 ~ He said, "Come." So Peter got out of the boat and walked on the water and came to Jesus. But when he saw the wind, he was afraid, and beginning to sink he cried out, "Lord, save me." Jesus immediately reached out his hand and took hold of him, saying to him, "O you of little faith, why did you doubt?" And when they got into the boat, the wind ceased.

The other morning I was sitting in my car beside the river, and I was angry. I was replaying a conversation a friend and I recently had and my mind was consumed with the hurtful things I'd heard and felt. I was grumpy at the state of the world... grumpy for things being so inconvenient and difficult right now... grumpy that things are just not going the way I want them to go!

And as I sat there consumed in my grumpitude, all I heard was noise.

It was deafening.

The cars rushing to and fro… the diesels roaring by, belching out suffocating fumes as they passed… the banging of the nearby construction site… the pounding of the thoughts as they ricocheted off the walls in my mind. It was too much! I was beginning to sink so, like Peter on the waves, I cried out, "Lord, save me!"

He didn't reach out and physically grab me like He did Peter, but He did immediately grab my attention with three little words.

"Fix your focus."

The words struck me, so I stopped for a moment and closed my eyes. I silenced the thoughts in my brain. I took a few deep breaths and felt how fresh the air really was. I stilled my angry heart and shut out the sounds of the world, just listening to my breath for a few. In the stillness of my breathing He gently repeated, "Just like Peter, you need to fix your focus."

I opened my eyes and looked around.

It was a glorious morning… the sun was glistening off the water, the geese were drifting lazily in the current, the birds were chattering in the branches above me, and two squirrels were scampering up and down the trunks and through the branches of the trees in a frenetic game of tag. My heart began to breathe as I allowed the peaceful splendor of the morning to soak deep into my core. The traffic and construction were still there, but as I brought my attention back to the birds and the beauty… everything else faded.

The Lord continued to breathe into my heart.

"Whatever you focus on becomes stronger. If you focus on your pain, it becomes more intense. When you focus on our lack, you see more of what you don't have. When you focus on your loneliness or your brokenness or your failings, giving them your power and energy and attention, then you rob yourself of the strength to step into something better. When you focus your heart on Me, you will have perfect peace." (Isaiah 26:3, Phil 4:6-7)

This is a fallen world, and in it we WILL have trouble. There will always be mean, selfish, hurtful people. There will always be arrogant co-workers, careless drivers, vicious politicians, annoying relatives, backbiting friends, frustrating (and even frightening!) troubles of many kinds. BUT… we get to choose whether or not to give them power and allow them to steal our joy, by giving them our focus.

Paul reminds us, "…whatever is true, whatever is worthy of reverence and is honorable and seemly, whatever is just, whatever is pure, whatever is lovely and lovable, whatever is kind and winsome and gracious, if there is any virtue and excellence, if there is anything worthy of praise, think on and weigh and take account of these things. Fix your minds on them." (Philippians 4:8)

Some translations say, "Let your mind dwell on these things." To "dwell" means to LIVE there. Yes, we go through the bad… we go THROUGH the Valley of the Shadow of Death… (Psalm 23) but we go THROUGH it. We don't dwell there. This is why Paul implores us to DWELL on THESE things instead. Yes, in this world the "bad" is always there, and while it's oftentimes easier to see, the good is easier to look at… and when you focus on the good, the bad becomes blurry!

One of my favorite verses in the Bible is from the prophet Isaiah who says, "You will keep him in perfect peace whose mind is fixed on You, because he trusts You." (Isaiah 26:3) Amen.

Oh, Lord... please help us to dwell in Your perfect peace by keeping our minds fixed on YOU. Moment by moment, breath by breath, each and every day of our lives. And when we start to sink into the negative... when we start to focus on the wind and the waves that threaten to drown us in our lives, please save us by grabbing us immediately like you did Peter, and bring us back to Your perfect peace... found only in You. Always. In Jesus' name we pray. Amen.

SCRIPTURES

Matthew 14:29-32 (ESV) ~ He said, "Come." So Peter got out of the boat and walked on the water and came to Jesus. But when he saw the wind, he was afraid, and beginning to sink he cried out, "Lord, save me." Jesus immediately reached out his hand and took hold of him, saying to him, "O you of little faith, why did you doubt?" And when they got into the boat, the wind ceased.

Isaiah 26:3-4 - You will guard him and keep him in perfect and constant peace whose mind [both its inclination and its character] is stayed on You, because he commits himself to You, leans on You, and hopes confidently in You. So trust in the Lord (commit yourself to Him, lean on Him, hope confidently in Him) forever; for the Lord God is an everlasting Rock [the Rock of Ages]. (AMP)

Phil 4:6-7 (NLT) ~ Don't worry about anything; instead, pray about everything. Tell God what you need, and thank him for all he has done. Then you will experience God's peace, which exceeds anything we can understand. His peace will guard your hearts and minds as you live in Christ Jesus.

Philippians 4:8 (AMPC) - For the rest, brethren, whatever is true, whatever is worthy of reverence and is honorable and seemly, whatever is just, whatever is pure, whatever is lovely and lovable, whatever is kind and winsome and gracious, if there is any virtue and excellence, if there is anything worthy of praise, think on and weigh and take account of these things. Fix your minds on them.

IN HIM

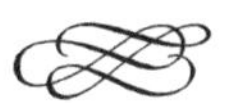

IN HIM WE LIVE AND MOVE AND HAVE OUR BEING

Key Scripture ~ Acts 17:28 ~ In Him we live and move and have our being.

We in He.

He is air
without which we would die
immediately
yet we take it for granted
always there
everywhere
but never seen

He is soil
rich

fertile
full of life
if we would but sink
our roots deep
but
this takes
time
this takes
stillness

He is the sun
provider of life
and warmth
and wellbeing
reflected
in nightly wanderers
and moonlight
guiding and
faithful each day

He is water
cool
and refreshing
in a blistering hot life
cleansing
and running over
fathomless depths
that beckon to deep

our fallow soil
broken up
our parched spirit
soaking up
the Seed of redemption
planted deep inside
a tiny shoot
following the sun
roots seeking
the depths
of His word
growing upwards
ever upwards
ever growing
slowly
growing
perfectly
always
in Him.
Amen.

LET'S FIND OUT!

WHAT WOULD HAPPEN IF WE ACTUALLY TRUSTED JESUS?

Key Scripture ~ Matthew 14:29-32 ~ He said, "Come." So Peter got out of the boat and walked on the water and came to Jesus. But when he saw the wind, he was afraid, and beginning to sink he cried out, "Lord, save me." Jesus immediately reached out his hand and took hold of him, saying to him, "O you of little faith, why did you doubt?" And when they got into the boat, the wind ceased.

I seem to refer to this key scripture a lot ... probably because I am sooooo like Peter!

Let's review the story. The disciples are in the midst of a terrible storm, in a boat without Jesus and they're doing everything they can to reach the shore. Suddenly they see Jesus walking on the water... and they all completely freak out. Jesus tells them it's Him and not to be afraid, and Peter basically says, "If it's really you, then let me come out to you!" Jesus says, "Come."

Now... let's just pause right there for a minute.

Do you think Jesus would say, "Come," just to have Peter get out of the boat and sink to his death? I mean, I guess he COULD have... but... seriously? That doesn't sound like God's heart to me.

No, I think Jesus wanted to give Peter a gift, so He invited Him to receive it. He said, "Come."

We all know what happens next... Peter gets out of the boat, starts walking (on the water!) towards Jesus, but then looks away from Jesus to the wind and the waves, is reminded of his fears, freaks out again, and starts to sink. Only then does he look back to Jesus and cry out, "Lord, save me!" Of course, Jesus immediately does, and then He asks Peter, "Why did you doubt?" Maybe I'm reading too much into it, but it sounds like Jesus is REALLY disappointed here... like, "Awww man! Why did you doubt? I had SUCH an awesome gift for you!"

Imagine for a moment what MAY have happened if Peter had kept his eyes on Jesus, and walked all the way to where Jesus was...

... maybe the storm would have cleared immediately, right then, instead of when they got back into the boat.

... maybe all the other disciples would have seen it was possible, and they would have gotten out of the boat and been able to receive the gift of walking on the water, too.

... maybe they would have all had a game of tag in the now warm sunshine on the shimmering surface of the lake.

I know, it's far-fetched... but... is it? Can you imagine it? Can you imagine the joy of God's heart seeing His children frolicking in His gift?

Poor Peter get's such a bad rap. I mean, if ONLY he'd kept his eyes on Jesus, right? But, I didn't hear any of the other disciples asking to join Jesus on the water. I know I sure wouldn't have! This is where I would NOT be like Peter! I probably would have been cowering in the bottom of the boat, clinging white-knuckled to the sides, weeping uncontrollably, screaming, "We're all gonna diiiiiiiie!!"

Not Peter.

He was daring... if even just for a moment.

What are WE afraid of in this storm? God tells us He will never leave us or forsake us, (Deuteronomy 31:6) that He will be with us always, even to the end of the age, (Matthew 28:20) and that He has GOOD plans for us. (Jeremiah 29:11)

Then, why are we so afraid of receiving His gifts?

Is it because we are focused on the wind and the waves, instead of on Him?

What are the wind and the waves in our storm? What are we afraid of right now?

Is it that we have too much to lose? That it will cost us too much? Too much time, too much money, too much energy, too much strength.... too much faith? Or like in Peter's case, it might cost us everything... we're afraid it might kill us?

Or, is it because we must let go of control? We must let go of the boat in order to take a step of faith... and trust?

What would it look like if we trusted?

What if we climbed over the side of the boat?

What if we stepped out onto the frigid water?

What if we let go of the boat (whatever that represents for each of us right now,) and dared to take a few faltering steps of faith towards Jesus?

What if we kept our eyes (and hearts and spirits) fixed on Him and His Word and His promises?

What would our lives look like then?

What would our lives look like if we trusted Him enough to receive the gifts He holds out for us?

And who else would be blessed by seeing us walking on the water with Jesus??!!

Let's find out!

Together!!

In Jesus, name.

Amen.

SCRIPTURES

Deuteronomy 31:6 ~ Be strong and courageous. Do not be afraid or terrified because of them, for the Lord your God goes with you; he will never leave you nor forsake you. (NIV)

Matthew 28:20 ~ I am with you always, even to the end of the age. (NASB)

Jeremiah 29:11 ~ For I know the plans I have for you," says the Lord. "They are plans for good and not for disaster, to give you a future and a hope. (NLT)

PATIENCE IN THE PAUSE

FINDING PEACE IN THE PAUSES OF YOUR LIFE

Your heart is never stopping. Until you're dead, of course, but it beats continuously throughout your day, throughout your life. Without stopping. I read somewhere that your heart actually rests in between each beat. In the pause.

I hate pausing for anything. It seems I am always on the go, doing something… usually until I drop from exhaustion. My mom says I suffer from the "go, go, go, collapse" syndrome. It's not that I don't take time to rest, at night or on the weekend or on vacation - when I'm "supposed" to, but when life (God) forces me to pause when I don't feel like I'm "supposed" to, or when I don't WANT to… I HATE it.

This is why God doesn't give me many details about my future. If He says, "We're going to that mountain over there," I take off in a full-out sprint towards the mountain. But, I never go the right way… I end up falling off cliffs and bogged down in swamps and drowning in rivers I was never supposed to wade into. It's usually only when I'm bruised and battered and worn out that I stop and realize, I've left

God behind. He never told me to go this way. If I sit and be still long enough, He comes up and sits down beside me.

"I'm sorry," I say. "I thought this was the way."

"Shhhhh," He gently whispers, stroking my hair and putting His arm around my shoulders. "Be still and know that *I* am God. My ways are not your ways," He says, smiling. "Would you like to try MY way now?"

When I take His hand and I follow Him He leads me in ways I never would have chosen. Down beautiful, awesome, and sometimes terrifying paths, but He's always with me.

The trouble is my will never wants to pause. I'm always focused on how far away the mountain seems, and I'm always anxious to be on my way. I want to GET there!!! But, that's not His way. We've all heard the tired cliche, "Life is a journey, not a destination." Yeah, yeah... blah, blah, blah... c'mon... let's GO!!! *laughing* When I shared this with a pastor friend of mine he told me, "That's not how God works. God is old and He's slow."

A muscle doesn't get stronger when it's being used... when you're running or lifting weights or doing push-ups your muscles are actually being stretched and literally torn down. It's when you stop exercising - in the pause - that your body rebuilds the muscle and makes it stronger. And then we tear it down again by exercising again and it's made stronger again when we rest again... and the cycle continues. My muscles don't usually hurt when I'm exercising. Sure, there's the burn, but it's the next day (or two or three!) - in the pause - that I'm sore.

Just like in my life. I feel great when I feel like I'm accomplishing things and moving forward and making progress. In the pause, I'm sore. But without the pause, I don't just "feel the burn" of accomplishment, I can literally burn out. There's only the constant tearing down and no real rebuilding.

Obviously, God has other plans for our lives than for us to just race to the end. It's in the pauses that He embraces us. (If we let Him.) It's when we're still that He reminds us that HE is God. It's in the pauses that we can catch our breath and absorb what He's been teaching us. It's in the pause that we truly grow. If we're patient… in Him.

SCRIPTURES

Psalm 46:10 ~ Be still and know that I am God.

Acts 17:28 ~ For in him we live and move and have our being.

1 Kings 19:11-12 ~ The Lord said, "Go out and stand on the mountain in the presence of the Lord, for the Lord is about to pass by." Then a great and powerful wind tore the mountains apart and shattered the rocks before the Lord, but the Lord was not in the wind. After the wind there was an earthquake, but the Lord was not in the earthquake. After the earthquake came a fire, but the Lord was not in the fire. And after the fire came a gentle whisper.

RANDOM BEAUTY

EVERYWHERE. EVERY DAY.

Thank you, Lord, for
random beauty.

Sunflowers on the side
of a dry, hot, dusty road.

A hawk soaring
just overhead
close enough to see
the pattern of it's feathers.

Cloud formations
that look like
turtles.

. . .

Itty bitty
puppy breath.

A quiet pine forest
flocked in snow.

A kitten's purr.

A warm smile.
Shared.

A kind gesture.

A gentle word.

A loving hug.

A child's laugh

somewhere in the store
a few aisles over.

Thank You, Lord.

Please make me
more
aware
of the random beauty
You sprinkle
my day with.

Every day.

In Jesus' name.

Amen.

SELF-CARE IS NOT SELF-ISH

THE IMPORTANCE OF TAKING CARE OF YOURSELF

Key Scripture ~ Mark 6:31 ~ "Come away to a quiet place and rest."

So often I see and hear Christians that are absolutely exhausted. They're tired, frazzled, and running from one thing to another without taking a breath. They seem to think the more they do, the closer they'll be to God.

I think it's actually the opposite.

I think the LESS we do, the MORE we can have space to do what HE wants us to do.

When I talk with people about this, I usually hear the same thing. They don't want to be selfish.

"I can't take the day off, that would be selfish..."

"I can't buy that for myself, that would be selfish..."

"I can't take a nap, that would be selfish..."

"I can't say no, that would be selfish..."

What we are failing to realize is that self care is NOT selfISH!

For example...

When we're flying in an airplane, before we get very far the flight attendant comes on and goes over all the safety instructions. Most people completely ignore them. They're reading or watching something or talking or sleeping... but I think there is a critical message that can be taken from these safety instructions.

"In the highly unlikely event that the cabin loses pressure, an oxygen mask will be released from a compartment above. Pull the mask down and place it over your nose and mouth. Though the bag will not inflate, oxygen IS flowing into the mask. SECURE YOUR OWN MASK BEFORE ASSISTING OTHERS..."

Three things...

1. We may not THINK doing this little thing, (taking care of ourselves in a small way,) is going to make a difference. We don't SEE the mask inflating... but we must TRUST that when we put the mask on, (and do something to take care of ourselves,) it WILL help us.
2. We MUST take care of ourselves FIRST! If we don't put OUR mask on first, then we may lose consciousness (and possibly die!) and then the little old lady or the child or the other person struggling that we COULD have helped, will probably die too, because we weren't able to help them... because we didn't take care of ourselves first!
3. Check your motives. Are you buying the new car because it's awesome and you want everyone to see

> you driving it? (Selfish.) Or, are you buying it because it has excellent safety and comfort ratings and you have spine issues that makes it painful for you to drive most other vehicles with lesser ratings? (Self care.)

Obviously, I am not advocating a “me first,” mentality in that we always think of ourselves first and disregard the needs of others. I’m saying we have to do the little things to take care of ourselves SO THAT we can then help others.

Jesus did this ALL the time, and He was obviously NOT selfish.

He would go off early in the morning and spend time praying. And He knew that His disciples needed this as well. In Mark 6:30-32 we read, “The apostles gathered together with Jesus; and they reported to Him all that they had done and taught. And He said to them, “Come away by yourselves to a secluded place and rest a little while.” (For there were many people coming and going, and they did not even have time to eat.) And they went away in the boat to a secluded place by themselves.”

As one of His disciples, He knows all that you are doing, and He whispers these words to your heart today... just as He did to His disciples long ago.

Take the time to care for yourself... and to allow Him to care for you. To fill you up so you are full of all that you need to carry out what He has planned for you to do.

Self care is actually the OPPOSITE of selfish.

In Him.

Always.

Amen.

SOCIAL DISTANCING

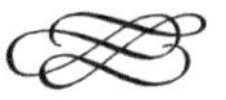

LET US RE-MEMBER!

THIS ARTICLE WAS WRITTEN DURING THE GLOBAL PANDEMIC OF 2020. IT HAS BEEN INCLUDED IN THIS COLLECTION AS IT STILL HAS SOME RELEVANCE IN OUR DAILY LIFE EVEN WHEN WE'RE NOT IN THE MIDST OF A PANDEMIC.

* * *

I'm having a really hard time right now, especially with this "social distancing". First of all, I don't think it's from God.

Don't get me wrong - I totally get that this virus is real, (as I type this I have a very dear friend in the ICU with this virus, fighting for his life!) and it's important for us all to practice safe habits… but God did not intend for us to be isolated from each other. (Genesis 2:18) The enemy loves to divide us - it's what he's been doing since the garden, (when the blame game started! Genesis 3:12-13) and we've all heard the phrase, "United we stand, divided we fall." It's true! We are always stronger when we're TOGETHER! (Ecclesiastes 4:12)

So, during this time when we are forced to isolate, and not get too near each other and not meet in groups and all the other ways we need to stay apart... how can we come together?

I think we need to re-member.

Let me explain.

I used to work for a hospital that had an amazing group of physicians (The Buncke Clinic) where they specialize in microsurgery. Seriously... they actually perform surgeries using microscopes so they can reattach body parts that had been dis-membered... fingers, toes, tongues, etc. They're experts at re-membering!!!

Paul said we are all members of one body, (1 Corinthians 12:12) and this social distancing is dis-membering us! Its separating members - members of church bodies, members of Bible studies, members of sewing groups and book clubs and even in some cases, families! If one part of the body is sick, it affects the whole body (1 Corinthians 12:26) so it's important for us to re-member each other!

But, how do we do this without being "non-compliant" to the social distancing rules?

First, again, I think we need to remember...

Remember what it was like to actually CALL someone on the phone and have a conversation! Not just shoot a text, but actually dial their phone number and SPEAK with them... hear their voice and let them hear your voice... and your heart.

Remember what it was like to hand-write a letter! Sanitize your hands first, and then handwrite a letter or card to someone you know would like to receive it. My 93 year old grandmother can't read the cards or letters she gets, but she LOVES getting them anyway - even if my mom has to read them aloud to her! A handwritten note seems to be a thing of the past, and yet when you take the time (which everyone seems to have a lot of right now!) to sit down and actually WRITE a note, it speaks volumes. Even more than the words on the page that you've written.

Remember what it was like to chat with your neighbor over the fence. You can stay far enough apart to not infect each other, yet still spread joy and love to one another by connecting in a nice conversation.

Remember what it was like to go for a walk. Outside. In the fresh air. And at least SMILE from a distance to passers-by, maybe even wave and say, "Hi!"! Even while keeping our distance from others, we don't need to treat them as lepers. (Sadly, I've actually seen this behavior taking place.) Remember, we're all going through this together, so let's be kind to each other and treat others the way we'd like to be treated. (Luke 6:31)

Remember that God uses all things for good. (Romans 8:28) He gave us a brain and a heart, so ask Him to take this bad situation and use it for good and help us think of NEW ways of connecting with each other. Try a "wagon wheel meeting" where we get some people and we all meet in an empty parking lot, (like at church!) and back our cars into a circle - like the spokes of a wagon wheel - open our back hatches and sit in the backs of our cars and chat for a while! Let's not let the enemy dis-member our body! Especially re-member those who may be more disconnected than others... elderly, widows, single parents... we know who they are... let's re-member them.

And last but not least, remember God. Keep your mind fixed on Him. (Isaiah 26:3) Remember to pray to Him continually. (Philippians 4:6-7) And remember that He loves you. He loves this WHOLE WORLD, (John 3:16-17) and He has a plan. A GOOD plan. (Jeremiah 29:11)

Even when it's hard.

Even when we're struggling.

Even when it seems like all is lost... its NOT!

Remember that.

In Jesus' name. Amen.

SCRIPTURES

Genesis 2:18 - NIV - The Lord God said, "It is not good for the man to be alone..."

Genesis 3:12-13 - ESV - The man said, "The woman whom you gave to be with me, she gave me fruit of the tree, and I ate." Then the Lord God said to the woman, "What is this that you have done?" The woman said, "The serpent deceived me, and I ate."

Ecclesiastes 4:12 - NLT - A person standing alone can be attacked and defeated, but two can stand back-to-back and conquer. Three are even better, for a triple-braided cord is not easily broken.

1 Corinthians 12:12 & 14 - NET - For just as the body is one and yet has many members, and all the members of the body —though many—are one body, so too is Christ... For in fact the body is not a single member, but many.

1 Corinthians 12:26 - ESV - If one member suffers, all suffer together;

Luke 6:31 - AMP - And as you would like and desire that men would do to you, do exactly so to them.

Romans 8:28 - NKJV - And we know that all things work together for good to those who love God, to those who are the called according to His purpose.

Isaiah 26:3 - NLT - You will keep in perfect peace all who trust in you, all whose thoughts are fixed on you!

Philippians 4:6-7 - ESV - Do not be anxious about anything, but in everything by prayer and supplication with thanksgiving let your requests be made known to God. And the peace of God, which surpasses all understanding, will guard your hearts and your minds in Christ Jesus.

John 3:16-17 - NET - For this is the way God loved the world: He gave his one and only Son, so that everyone who believes in him will not perish but have eternal life. For God did not send his Son into the world to condemn the world, but that the world should be saved through him.

Jeremiah 29:11 - NIV - For I know the plans I have for you," declares the Lord, "plans to prosper you and not to harm you, plans to give you hope and a future.

THE JOY OF GIVING YOUR GIFTS AWAY

WE'RE GIVEN GIFTS TO SHARE THEM!

K*ey Scripture* ~ *Ephesians 2:10 ~ For we are God's masterpiece. He has created us anew in Christ Jesus, so we can do the good things he planned for us long ago. Amplified - For we are His workmanship [His own master work, a work of art], created in Christ Jesus [reborn from above—spiritually transformed, renewed, ready to be used] for good works, which God prepared [for us] beforehand [taking paths which He set], so that we would walk in them [living the good life which He prearranged and made ready for us].* AMEN!!!

Let me start by clarifying something… "joy" is different than "happiness." I'm "happy" when it's a warm summer day and I'm walking on the beach with my husband, (basically when things are going MY way!) and I'm grumpy when they're NOT! But, I can have JOY all the time. Paul wrote the his letter to the Philippians while in prison, and that book is filled with the word JOY.

Why? How is this possible?

Because, even in prison, Paul had the joy of Jesus in his heart and he was doing what Jesus had called him to do.

As we just read in Ephesians, God has given each of us gifts - gifts that are unique to us. Maybe it's cooking, or cleaning, or teaching, or singing, or encouraging, or healing.... whatever it is that you love to do, even when nobody else knows you're doing it. You HAVE to do it... if you stop for too long, you start to twitch... it's like something is off in your soul.

Way back in the Old Testament, one of God's prophets, Jeremiah, was discouraged that nobody was listening to him... so he gave up and decided he wasn't going to speak about God anymore! But after a while, he said he felt like there was a fire in his bones. (Jeremiah 20:9) He couldn't help it! He HAD to do what God had created him to do.

And so do you!

In addition, our joy will always be amplified when we're using our gifts to help others, because God lives and works THROUGH us. Even a paraplegic can be a powerful prayer warrior or even a motivational speaker like Nick Vujicic!

If you have a pulse - you have a purpose! And the amazing thing, (and as Rick Warren points out - in fact, he actually STARTS his "Purpose Driven Life" book by saying,) it's not about YOU.

Yes, it's OUR joy, but God calls us to follow Him so we can experience joy WITH Him. And believe me, His will for us is ALWAYS greater than ours. (He's like the mighty ocean and we usually go to Him with a thimble-sized cup to be filled. He's like, "Seriously?!!")

Why did He create us? Why did He plan things for us to do?? He doesn't NEED us. HE'S GOD!

It's because He LOVES us. He invites us to partner with Him and experience His joy WITH Him., so we can be BLESSED… with Him!

Yes, the awesome thing about the gifts He's given us, (and what truly shows the heart of God,) is that these gifts are not JUST for us… they're for us to give away!

If we love to bake, and we just bake cookies for ourselves, that's nice… but it's AWESOME when we give those cookies away! (And then others LOVE us, too! Ha!) (Acts 20:35)

When we share our gifts with others, it brings joy to us, it brings joy to others… and it brings joy to God! A trinity … a cord of 3, not easily broken, binding us all together in relationship! (Ecclesiastes 4:12)

He gives us our gifts and includes us in His work not as a burden, but as a blessing!

So follow Him in your joy!

Don't think you don't have something to give? You DO! Again, if you have a pulse, you have a purpose. If you really want to experience true joy in your life, ask God how you can give away the gifts He's given you. Ask Him to use you according to His will for your life… and then buckle in - because He will!!!

SCRIPTURES

Ephesians 2:10 ~ For we are His workmanship [His own master work, a work of art], created in Christ Jesus [reborn from above—spiritually transformed, renewed, ready to be used] for good works, which God prepared [for us] beforehand [taking paths which He set], so that we would walk in them [living the good life which He prearranged and made ready for us]. (AMP)

Philippians 4:4 ~ Always be full of joy in the Lord. I say it again—rejoice! (NLT)

Jeremiah 20:9 - But if I say, "I will not mention his word or speak anymore in his name," his word is in my heart like a fire, a fire shut up in my bones. I am weary of holding it in; indeed, I cannot.

Acts 20:35 ~ In all things I have shown you that by working hard in this way we must help the weak and remember the words of the Lord Jesus, how he himself said, 'It is more blessed to give than to receive. (ESV)

Ecclesiastes 4:12 ~ By yourself you're unprotected. With a friend you can face the worst. Can you round up a third? A three-stranded rope isn't easily snapped. (MSG)

WHY DON'T I SEE GOD?

MAYBE YOU JUST DON'T REALIZE IT'S HIM...

K*ey Scripture:* ***Romans 1:19-20*** ~ *This is because what is known about God should be plain to them because God made it plain to them. Ever since the creation of the world, God's invisible qualities—God's eternal power and divine nature—have been clearly seen, because they are understood through the things God has made. So humans are without excuse. (CEB)*

Once upon a time there were two brothers, Ciego and Miveen. Ciego and Miveen led very similar lives... but they saw things in very different ways.

❖

Ciego and Miveen grew up with very little - little food, little money, little love - and their parents were really dysfunctional...

. . .

Ciego saw how other kids lived and always wished he could be them. He saw how other kids had what he wanted, and to him, it just wasn't fair. He hated his family and felt that everyone and everything was against him. Life was hard and it sucked.

Miveen saw how other kids lived and wondered why their life was different. He watched their parents and it was often in stark contrast to his own. He saw how hard his parents struggled, and he thought that must be why they were so angry and abusive. Or maybe Gramma or Grampa were angry to them when they were little? He had some friends who had more things than he did, but he had other friends who had a lot less. He noticed there were others way worse off than he was, and he became grateful for the things he had.

❖

Ciego and Miveen both had to go to Sunday school at church...

Ciego thought it was just a bunch of silly fantasy and fairy tales. Everyone knows people can't walk on water or be raised from the dead. He saw how some of the people at church behaved... how they treated each other badly, talked about each other behind each others' backs... and it seemed like they weren't any better than people who DIDN'T go to church. Besides, if God was supposed to be "our Father," then He was probably just a bigger, badder version of his own father... and he wanted no part of that!!!

. . .

Miveen loved the stories of Jesus. How Jesus loved little children, and treated everyone with love and kindness and respect... even when others said they were really bad, Jesus still loved them. Miveen thought Jesus and Jesus' Father must be really loving, because even when he, and the others in the church, messed up and behaved badly, Jesus still loved them and forgave them. That's the kind of Father he knew he needed.

❖

Ciego and Miveen were able to join the Boy Scouts...

Ciego loved going on the camping trips as it was an opportunity to be away from his parents and to be as wild and free as he could be. On the hikes he would run through the forest screaming and scaring as many things as he could - including the troop leaders!

Miveen loved going on the camping trips as it was a time for him to be away from his troubled home life as well. He loved the quiet of the forest, (when there weren't others running screaming through it!) and thanked God for the beauty he saw in the trees and the plants and the animals. He loved the stillness of the lake in the morning, and could feel God's presence more easily here than anywhere else.

. . .

❖

The boys grew into men, and both got jobs at the same company, got married, and had children.

Ciego's wife was a beautiful woman... but he still thought a lot about that hot little redhead at work, and how she reminded him of that actress in that movie.

Miveen also married, and he thanked God every day for the gift that his wife was to him and to their family, and how her heart of service and love of God made her more and more beautiful every day.

❖

Ciego loved science, and only believed what could be seen with the eyes, heard with the ears, experienced with the 5 senses and scientifically proven. Period.

Miveen loved science as well, and he praised God for His wisdom in not only creating science, but also for His love in doing so... in designing science to automatically create beauty in all things, from rainbows when it rains, to rock formations, to ocean waves, to snowflakes, to fields of flowers seen from afar.

❖

Ciego and Miveen both got a pay raise at work.

Ciego felt it was about stinkin' time, though he was still upset that he wasn't making what he felt he SHOULD be making, or what he thought others probably made.

Miveen thanked God for His generous provision, and prayed that everything he did each day would be a reflection of God, and would therefore bring Him all the glory.

❖

Both men were very gifted and talented in their work.

Ciego was quick to say that nothing was handed to him… he was self-taught and had worked hard to earn everything he had. When he was disciplined, he was quick to blame others and argue how he wasn't at fault… even when deep down he knew there was some truth to what had been brought up.

Miveen saw his talents as gifts from God and therefore should be given away and shared. When he was disciplined, he would bring the rebuke before God in prayer and ask to be shown what was true in the correction, and how he could improve. He thanked God for all that he had been given, and prayed that God would make him into the man He created him to be, for others and for Him.

❖

Their company held a fundraiser to raise money for the poor.

Ciego wanted no part of it. He felt that he had to earn everything he had, so other people should, too… especially those drunks and drug addicts that should just get their act together and get a job.

Miveen remembered his childhood. He knew how a small change in the economy or his health or something else could be devastating to him and his family, so he did what he could to help the fundraiser, thinking, "There, but by the grace of God, go I…"

❖

When storm clouds were on the horizon and it looked to be a snowy, harsh, cold wintery day…

Ciego complained about having to scrape ice off his windshield, and how long it took his truck to warm up, and how he was probably going to have to drive all the way to work dealing with stupid drivers from another state that didn't know how to drive in the snow.

. . .

Miveen looked up and thanked God for the beautiful cloud formations, for the abundance of snow, especially in the mountains, that would fill the aquifers and provide the much needed water in the summer.

❖

On sleepless nights Ciego would toss and turn and his mind would continuously fret and churn.

Miveen would strike up a conversation with God, discussing and handing over his concerns, until sleep eventually tucked him in.

❖

One day Ciego and Miveen were discussing Jesus coming back. Ciego scoffed and said, "It's been over 2000 years and nothing's happened yet!" When Miveen replied, "God is being patient and is delaying His return to give people time to come to Him and be saved," Ciego retorted, "I'm a good person. I don't need to be saved by anyone. Besides, who wants to spend eternity playing a harp on some cloud?! I'd rather be partying it up with my friends down THERE!"

❖

. . .

One terrible year, their mother was in a horrific car accident. After numerous surgeries and months of rehab she passed away.

Ciego became bitter and angry. When anyone would come to see him or offer their condolences or just want to spend time with him, he would refuse to answer the door until they left, or would send them away, telling them he wanted to be left alone. He was furious with God. Where was He in all of this? He felt this was just proof that God didn't exist, and if He did, He certainly didn't care. If He was a loving God, why would He ever let something like this happen? Why would He let someone suffer like that, and die??

Miveen was completely devastated by the loss of his mother as well. He wrestled mightily with God, trying to understand the same questions Ciego had. As horrific the loss and as deep as the wound was, there was a part of him that was grateful to God that at least the suffering was over, and that his mother was now with Him. Through it all, he never felt alone or abandoned. He saw each person who came over or called or prayed for him and his family as being the hands and feet of Jesus. He knew that God wasn't going to show up in his living room, (although he desperately wished He would!) but that God DID show up in the living room when a neighbor brought over a meal, or when a family from church came by to see them, or when the phone rang and the person on the other end prayed for him. He slowly began to see that by going through this grueling experience, he could now better understand the pain of others, and could maybe help them go through similar things as well. And he knew that even though he couldn't understand it at all, that God was still good... that God did not make this happen... but He would use it for good, if Miveen would allow it.

❖

One day, shortly after their mother's death, while Miveen was leaving work he saw Ciego in the parking lot, just sitting in his car, so he walked over and knocked on the window. Ciego looked up at him and rolled the window down. Miveen could tell that Ciego had been crying.

"Hey Ciego, why don't you come over for dinner. I'm sure my wife wouldn't mind, and it would be good for us to have some time to talk." Ciego really didn't feel like it, and without knowing why, he slowly nodded his head and followed Miveen to his house.

During dinner the men talked about their lives and shared stories of their childhood. The mood was light, but there was a heaviness in the air. After dinner when it was time to leave, Ciego thanked them and Miveen walked him out.

They stood on the porch and Ciego looked like he really wanted to say something, so Miveen was silent and gave him the time and space he needed.

. . .

Finally, Ciego looked at Miveen with a pleading look on his face.

"What is it?" Miveen asked.

"I don't understand." Ciego answered.

Miveen felt there was more, so he looked at him gently and just waited. Ciego looked away and continued, "We grew up together. We've been through everything together. Our lives are so similar... and yet... they're completely different. God has blessed you, and He's cursed me. I don't understand. He loves you and He hates me. Why?"

"God doesn't hate you, Ciego." Miveen said softly.

"Yes He does. You see God everywhere," Ciego replied, "and I never see him."

"You see Him when bad things happen and you start railing against Him and blaming Him for the bad things," Miveen said, with a soft smile.

Ciego stared at his brother, trying to absorb what he'd said. "I don't understand," he said again. "I don't see God... if He were here right now, I'd give him a piece of my mind!"

. . .

"You DO see God. Everybody sees God, Ciego," Miveen answered softly. "He's everywhere. He's constantly revealing Himself, but people want Him to show up the way THEY want Him to. They want God to be what THEY want Him to be, and do what THEY want Him to do... but He's way bigger than that."

"I don't understand," Ciego repeated.

"You do see God," Miveen said again gently, putting his hand on his brother's shoulder. "You just don't realize that it's Him. You don't recognize Him, because you don't have a relationship with Him."

Ciego looked down and tears filled his eyes. "I've tried praying. He just doesn't answer."

"He's not a genie in a bottle you can summon by your prayers to do your bidding," Miveen answered. "He's a loving Father Who wants a RELATIONSHIP with you. More than just rocket prayers you shoot to heaven when you want something. He wants to spend time with you, to have you sit silently with Him and learn to hear His voice."

After a long time, Ciego sniffed and said softly, "I'd like that."

"It takes time," said Miveen. "Just as you can recognize my voice in a crowded room because of our relationship, you will begin to recognize His voice as well. You'll start to see His love in everything... and that's when you'll start to see HIM... not as some apparition in your living room, but as He truly is. In the love all around you."

Ciego looked at his brother with a softness that had never been there before. Then, he said, "Thank you, Miveen," and he hugged his brother, and left.

SCRIPTURES

Isaiah 55:9 ~ For as the heavens are higher than the earth, so are my ways higher than your ways and my thoughts than your thoughts. (ESV)

John 8:42 ~ Jesus replied, "If God were your Father, you would love me, for I have come from God and am now here..." (NET)

2 Corinthians 1:4 ~ He comforts us in all our troubles so that we can comfort others. When they are troubled, we will be able to give them the same comfort God has given us. (NLT)

Romans 1:19-20 ~ This is because what is known about God should be plain to them because God made it plain to them. Ever since the creation of the world, God's invisible qualities

—God's eternal power and divine nature—have been clearly seen, because they are understood through the things God has made. So humans are without excuse. (CEB)

ABOUT THE AUTHOR

Dart is the gifted and inspired creator of the website, aBranchOnTheVine.com. The site is a brilliant faith-based blog designed to help us know the uncomplicated truth about Jesus.

A Christian for most of her life who has overcome obstacles including mental, emotional, and physical traumas, Dart knows the Jesus she follows and is passionate about communicating His goodness to the world.

By day, Dart is the Manager of Learning & Development and Talent Management for a global outdoor recreation company. She spends her evenings serving the homeless in her community alongside the love of her life, John, who is the Director of a local non-profit, long-term rehabilitation organization, homeless shelter and navigation center.

Read more from Dart at aBranchOnTheVine.com, or send her an email at Dart@aBranchOnTheVine.com